If you can keep your head when all about you
Are losing theirs . . .
Rudyard Kipling

First published in Great Britain in 2019 by

Quercus Editions Ltd
Carmelite House
50 Victoria Embankment
London EC4Y 0DZ

An Hachette UK company

A CIP catalogue record for this book is available
from the British Library

ISBN 978 1 52940 283 4

10 9 8 7 6 5 4 3 2 1

Typeset by EM&EN Limited
Printed and bound in Great Britain by Clays Ltd, Elcograf S.p.A.

POEMS TO FIX A

F**ked Up

WORLD

Quercus

'This is not a poetry book as you know it,
this is a life raft.'
Emerald Street on *Poems for a world gone to sh*t*

Sometimes, you just need someone to tell you
things are going to be OK –
and that's the moment for poetry.

Poets know what it's like to feel like sh*t,
they're really good at putting it into words,
and they're better than anyone
at reminding you
that the world might be f**ked up,
but it's really f**king beautiful, too.

So here's a little collection of short poems and extracts
to help you put the sh*t in perspective:
work, adventure, wisdom, love, rest, purpose –
let the soothing balm of poetry help you
find your balance . . .

I

work

nursery rhyme

anon.

All work and no play makes Jack a dull boy;
All play and no work makes Jack a mere toy.

from *the prophet*
kahlil gibran

I say to you that when you work you fulfil a part of earth's furthest dream, assigned to you when that dream was born,

And in keeping yourself with labour you are in truth loving life,

And to love life through labour is to be intimate with life's inmost secret . . .

And what is it to work with love?

It is to weave the cloth with threads drawn from your heart, even as if your beloved were to wear that cloth.

It is to build a house with affection, even as if your beloved were to dwell in that house.

It is to sow seeds with tenderness and reap the harvest with joy, even as if your beloved were to eat the fruit.

It is to charge all things you fashion with a breath of your own spirit,

And to know that all the blessed dead are standing about you and watching . . .

Work is love made visible.

woman work
maya angelou

I've got the children to tend
The clothes to mend
The floor to mop
The food to shop
Then the chicken to fry
The baby to dry
I got company to feed
The garden to weed
I've got shirts to press
The tots to dress
The cane to be cut
I gotta clean up this hut
Then see about the sick
And the cotton to pick.

Shine on me, sunshine
Rain on me, rain
Fall softly, dewdrops
And cool my brow again.

Storm, blow me from here
With your fiercest wind
Let me float across the sky
'Til I can rest again.

Fall gently, snowflakes
Cover me with white
Cold icy kisses and
Let me rest tonight.

Sun, rain, curving sky
Mountain, oceans, leaf and stone
Star shine, moon glow
You're all that I can call my own.

Out in the garden,
Out in the windy, swinging dark,
Under the trees and over the flower-beds,
Over the grass and under the hedge border,
Someone is sweeping, sweeping,
Some old gardener.
Out in the windy, swinging dark
Someone is secretly putting in order,
Someone is creeping, creeping.

I tie my Hat – I crease my Shawl –
Life's little duties do – precisely –
As the very least
Were infinite – to me –

I put new Blossoms in the Glass –
And throw the old – away –
I push a petal from my Gown
That anchored there – I weigh
The time 'twill be till six o'clock
I have so much to do –
And yet – Existence – some way back –
Stopped – struck – my ticking – through –
We cannot put Ourself away
As a completed Man
Or Woman – When the Errand's done
We came to Flesh – upon –

There may be – Miles on Miles of Nought –
Of Action – sicker far –
To simulate – is stinging work –
To cover what we are
From Science – and from Surgery –
Too Telescopic Eyes
To bear on us unshaded –
For their – sake – not for Ours –
'Twould start them –
We – could tremble –
But since we got a Bomb –
And held it in our Bosom –
Nay – Hold it – it is calm –

Therefore – we do life's labor –
Though life's Reward – be done –
With scrupulous exactness –
To hold our Senses – on –

If the girl who made your skirt's not paid
you cannot say it's beautiful
if the pay is less than living wage
you cannot say it's beautiful
if the coloured dyes now lie in rivers
poisoned fish, polluted waters
if there's no sick pay, no toilet breaks
if the factories are in decay
no matter what your mirror says
or how stylish you might look today
you cannot claim it's beautiful

Last night when my work was done,
And my estranged hands
Were becoming mutually interested
In such forgotten things as pulses,
I looked out of a window
Into a glittering night sky.

And instantly
I began to feather-stitch a ring around the moon.

There was an old woman tossed up in a basket,
Seventeen times as high as the moon;
Where she was going I couldn't but ask it,
For in her hand she carried a broom.
Old woman, old woman, old woman, quoth I,
Where are you going to up so high?
To brush the cobwebs off the sky!
May I go with you? Aye, by-and-by.

Dust if you must, but wouldn't it be better
To paint a picture or write a letter,
Bake a cake or plant a seed,
Ponder the difference between want and need?

Dust if you must, but there's not much time,
With rivers to swim, and mountains to climb,
Music to hear and books to read,
Friends to cherish and life to lead.

Dust if you must, but the world's out there,
With the sun in your eyes, the wind in your hair,
A flutter of snow, a shower of rain.
This day will not come around again.

Dust if you must, but bear in mind,
Old age will come and it's not kind.
And when you go – and go you must –
You, yourself, will make more dust.

When I had money, money, O!
My many friends proved all untrue;
But now I have no money, O!
My friends are real, though very few.

II

adventure

It is a pleasant thing to roam abroad,
And gaze on scenes and objects strange and grand;
To sail in mighty ships o'er distant seas,
And roam the mountains of a foreign land.

Afoot and light-hearted I take to the open road,
Healthy, free, the world before me,
The long brown path before me leading wherever
       I choose.

Henceforth I ask not good-fortune, I myself am
       good-fortune,
Henceforth I whimper no more, postpone no more,
       need nothing,
Done with indoor complaints, libraries, querulous
       criticisms,
Strong and content I travel the open road.

I saw a peacock with a fiery tail
I saw a blazing comet drop down hail
I saw a cloud with ivy circled round
I saw a sturdy oak creep on the ground
I saw a pismire swallow up a whale
I saw a raging sea brim full of ale
I saw a Venice glass sixteen foot deep
I saw a well full of men's tears that weep
I saw their eyes all in a flame of fire
I saw a house as big as the moon and higher
I saw the sun even in the midst of night
I saw the man that saw this wondrous sight.

Faster than fairies, faster than witches,
Bridges and houses, hedges and ditches;
And charging along like troops in a battle,
All through the meadows the horses and cattle:
All of the sights of the hill and the plain
Fly as thick as driving rain;
And ever again, in the wink of an eye,
Painted stations whistle by.

Here is a child who clambers and scrambles,
All by himself and gathering brambles;
Here is a tramp who stands and gazes;
And there is the green for stringing the daisies!
Here is a cart run away in the road
Lumping along with man and load;
And here is a mill and there is a river:
Each a glimpse and gone for ever!

Now there is nothing gives a man such spirits,
　　　　Leavening his blood as cayenne doth a curry,
As going at full speed – no matter where its
　　　　Direction be, so 'tis but in a hurry,
And merely for the sake of its own merits;
　　　　For the less cause there is for all this flurry,
The greater is the pleasure in arriving
And the great *end* of travel – which is driving.

. . . And when I think upon a pot of beer –
　　　　But I won't weep! – and so drive on, postilions!
As the smart boys spurred fast in their career,
　　　　Juan admired these highways of free millions,
A country in all senses the most dear
　　　　To foreigner or native, save some silly ones,
Who 'kick against the pricks' just at this juncture,
And for their pains get only a fresh puncture.

I started Early – Took my Dog –
And visited the Sea –
The Mermaids in the Basement
Came out to look at me –

And Frigates – in the Upper Floor
Extended Hempen Hands –
Presuming Me to be a Mouse –
Aground – upon the Sands –

But no Man moved Me – till the Tide
Went past my simple Shoe –
And past my Apron – and my Belt
And past my Bodice – too –

And made as He would eat me up –
As wholly as a Dew
Upon a Dandelion's Sleeve –
And then – I started – too –

And He – He followed – close behind –
I felt His Silver Heel
Upon my Ankle – Then my Shoes
Would overflow with Pearl –

Until We met the Solid Town –
No One He seemed to know –
And bowing – with a Mighty look –
At me – The Sea withdrew –

The tide rises, the tide falls,
The twilight darkens, the curlew calls;
Along the sea-sands damp and brown
The traveller hastens toward the town,
    And the tide rises, the tide falls.

Darkness settles on roofs and walls,
But the sea, the sea in the darkness calls;
The little waves, with their soft, white hands,
Efface the footprints in the sands,
    And the tide rises, the tide falls.

The morning breaks; the steeds in their stalls
Stamp and neigh, as the hostler calls;
The day returns, but nevermore
Returns the traveller to the shore,
    And the tide rises, the tide falls.

They went to sea in a Sieve, they did,
    In a Sieve they went to sea:
In spite of all their friends could say,
On a winter's morn, on a stormy day,
    In a Sieve they went to sea!
And when the Sieve turned round and round,
And every one cried, 'You'll all be drowned!'
They called aloud, 'Our Sieve ain't big,
But we don't care a button! we don't care a fig!
    In a Sieve we'll go to sea!'
      Far and few, far and few,
        Are the lands where the Jumblies live;
        Their heads are green, and their hands are blue,
        And they went to sea in a Sieve . . .

The water it soon came in, it did,
    The water it soon came in;
So to keep them dry, they wrapped their feet
In a pinky paper all folded neat,
    And they fastened it down with a pin.
And they passed the night in a crockery-jar,
And each of them said, 'How wise we are!
Though the sky be dark, and the voyage be long,
Yet we never can think we were rash or wrong,
    While round in our Sieve we spin!'

They sailed to the Western Sea, they did,
　　　To a land all covered with trees,
And they bought an Owl, and a useful Cart,
And a pound of Rice, and a Cranberry Tart,
　　　And a hive of silvery Bees.
And they bought a Pig, and some green Jack-daws,
And a lovely Monkey with lollipop paws,
And forty bottles of Ring-Bo-Ree,
　　　And no end of Stilton Cheese.

And in twenty years they all came back,
　　　In twenty years or more,
And every one said, 'How tall they've grown!
For they've been to the Lakes, and the Torrible Zone,
　　　And the hills of the Chankly Bore';
And they drank their health, and gave them a feast
Of dumplings made of beautiful yeast;
And every one said, 'If we only live,
We too will go to sea in a Sieve,—
　　　To the hills of the Chankly Bore!'
　　　　Far and few, far and few,
　　　　　Are the lands where the Jumblies live;
　　　　Their heads are green, and their hands are blue,
　　　　　And they went to sea in a Sieve.

Early in the day it was whispered that we should sail
          in a boat,
only thou and I, and never a soul in the world would
          know of this our
pilgrimage to no country and to no end.

In that shoreless ocean,
at thy silently listening smile my songs would swell
          in melodies,
free as waves, free from all bondage of words.

Is the time not come yet?
Are there works still to do?
Lo, the evening has come down upon the shore
and in the fading light the seabirds come flying to
          their nests.

Who knows when the chains will be off,
and the boat, like the last glimmer of sunset,
vanish into the night?

And the rains fall soft upon your fields

And until we meet again,

May the road rise to meet you,
May the wind be ever at your back
May the sun shine warm upon your face,
And the rains fall soft upon your fields.
And until we meet again,
May God hold you in the palm of his hand.

III

wisdom

No more wine? then we'll push back chairs and talk.

The proper way to eat a fig, in society,
Is to split it in four, holding it by the stump,
And open it, so that it is a glittering, rosy, moist, honied,
      heavy-petalled four-petalled flower.

Then you throw away the skin
Which is just like a four-sepalled calyx,
After you have taken off the blossom with your lips.

But the vulgar way
Is just to put your mouth to the crack, and take out the
      flesh in one bite.

Every fruit has its secret.

the tables turned
william wordsworth

Up! up! my friend, and clear your looks,
Why all this toil and trouble?
Up! up! my friend, and quit your books,
Or surely you'll grow double.

The sun above the mountain's head,
A freshening lustre mellow,
Through all the long green fields has spread,
His first sweet evening yellow.

Books! 'tis a dull and endless strife,
Come, hear the woodland linnet,
How sweet his music; on my life
There's more of wisdom in it.

And hark! how blithe the throstle sings!
He, too, is no mean preacher;
Come forth into the light of things,
Let Nature be your teacher.

She has a world of ready wealth,
Our minds and hearts to bless –
Spontaneous wisdom breathed by health,
Truth breathed by cheerfulness.

One impulse from a vernal wood
May teach you more of man,
Of moral evil and of good,
Than all the sages can.

Sweet is the lore which Nature brings;
Our meddling intellect
Misshapes the beauteous forms of things;
– We murder to dissect.

Enough of Science and of Art;
Close up those barren leaves;
Come forth, and bring with you a heart
That watches and receives.

To see a World in a Grain of Sand
And a Heaven in a Wild Flower,
Hold Infinity in the palm of your hand,
And Eternity in an hour.

I walked a mile with Pleasure;
She chattered all the way,
But left me none the wiser
For all she had to say.

I walked a mile with Sorrow
And ne'er a word said she;
But oh, the things I learned from her
When Sorrow walked with me!

Forgive yourself
for everything you broke
when you were trying to survive.

Let the rain
wash away
your regret.

Let your blood cool
from the rage
you feel against yourself.

Let the rivers
under your skin
bring you home.

To heal you must forgive
your heart, your skin, your body
all of their mistakes.

I saw Eternity the other night,
Like a great ring of pure and endless light,
    All calm, as it was bright;
And round beneath it, Time in hours, days, years,
    Driven by the spheres,
Like a vast shadow moved; in which the World
    And all her train were hurl'd.

There should be no despair for you
    While nightly stars are burning,
While evening pours its silent dew
    And sunshine gilds the morning.
There should be no despair – though tears
    May flow down like a river:
Are not the best beloved of years
    Around your heart for ever?

They weep, you weep, it must be so;
    Winds sigh as you are sighing,
And Winter sheds his grief in snow
    Where Autumn's leaves are lying:
Yet, these revive, and from their fate
    Your fate cannot be parted,
Then, journey on, if not elate,
    Still *never* broken-hearted!

Up here, with June, the sycamore throws
    Across the window a whispering screen;
I shall miss the sycamore more, I suppose,
Than anything else on this earth that is out in green.
    But I mean to go through the door without fear,
    Not caring much what happens here
      When I'm away: –
How green the screen is across the panes
    Or who goes laughing along the lanes
With my old lover all summer day.

from *as you like it*
william shakespeare

All the world's a stage,
And all the men and women merely players;
They have their exits and their entrances,
And one man in his time plays many parts,
His acts being seven ages. At first, the infant,
Mewling and puking in the nurse's arms.
Then the whining schoolboy, with his satchel
And shining morning face, creeping like snail
Unwillingly to school. And then the lover,
Sighing like furnace, with a woeful ballad
Made to his mistress' eyebrow. Then a soldier,
Full of strange oaths and bearded like the pard,
Jealous in honour, sudden and quick in quarrel,
Seeking the bubble reputation
Even in the cannon's mouth . . .

. . . And then the justice,
In fair round belly with good capon lined,
With eyes severe and beard of formal cut,
Full of wise saws and modern instances;
And so he plays his part. The sixth age shifts
Into the lean and slippered pantaloon,
With spectacles on nose and pouch on side;
His youthful hose, well saved, a world too wide
For his shrunk shank, and his big manly voice,
Turning again toward childish treble, pipes
And whistles in his sound. Last scene of all,
That ends this strange eventful history,
Is second childishness and mere oblivion,
Sans teeth, *sans* eyes, *sans* taste, *sans* everything.

IV

love

Love much. Earth has enough of bitter in it;
    Cast sweets into its cup whene'er you can.
No heart so hard, but love at last may win it;
    Love is the grand primeval cause of man;
    All hate is foreign to the first great plan.

Most people in your life
were only meant
for dreams,
and summer laughter.

They stay till the wind changes,
the tides turn,
or disappear
with the first snow.

And then there are some
that were forged
to weather blizzards
and pain with you.

They were cast in iron,
set in gold
and never ever leave you
to face anything alone.

Know who those people are.
And love them the way they deserve.
Not everyone in your life is temporary.
A few are as permanent as love is old.

The leaves talked in the twilight, dear;
    Hearken the tale they told:
How in some far-off place and year,
    Before the world grew old,

I was a dreaming forest tree,
    You were a wild, sweet bird
Who sheltered at the heart of me
    Because the north wind stirred;

How, when the chiding gale was still,
    When peace fell soft on fear,
You stayed one golden hour to fill
    My dream with singing, dear.

To-night the self-same songs are sung
    The first green forest heard;
My heart and the gray world grow young –
    To shelter you, my bird.

That you carried a cello on your back like a shell.

That you were the only pupil at school with a beard.

That your large shoulders hunched to write equations.

That you looked like someone who liked Sonic Youth.

That you struggled to hold chopsticks.

That Portuguese was your mother tongue.

That you wore glasses, thinking you were alone.

That you were leaning on a shelf of Swedish literature.

That you were balding and calm.

That you were on the floor, facing Mecca.

That you were buying clams.

That your aviators were a defence mechanism.

That I wanted to sleep with you immediately.

That you were wearing a black suit in a white art gallery.

That you were selling roses at night.

That there was something of Gavrilo Princip about you.

That I had met you the previous summer (untrue).

That you were dressed in drag as a bride.

That you were young and male among middle-aged women.

The clouds had made a crimson crown
    Above the mountains high.
The stormy sun was going down
    In a stormy sky.

Why did you let your eyes so rest on me,
    And hold your breath between?
In all the ages this can never be
    As if it had not been.

I wonder
how it would be here with you,
where the wind
that has shaken off its dust in low valleys
touches one cleanly
as with a new-washed hand,
and pain
is as the remote hunger of droning things,
and anger
but a little silence
sinking into the great silence.

Love is feeling cold in the back of vans
Love is a fanclub with only two fans
Love is walking holding paintstained hands
Love is

Love is fish and chips on winter nights
Love is blankets full of strange delights
Love is when you don't put out the light
Love is

Love is the presents in Christmas shops
Love is when you're feeling Top of the Pops
Love is what happens when the music stops
Love is

Love is white panties lying all forlorn
Love is a pink nightdress still slightly warm
Love is when you have to leave at dawn
Love is

Love is you and love is me
Love is a prison and love is free
Love's what's there when you're away from me
Love is . . .

The moth's kiss, first!
Kiss me as if you made believe
You were not sure, this eve,
How my face, your flower, had pursed
Its petals up; so here and there
You brush it, till I grow aware
Who wants me, and wide ope I burst.

The bee's kiss, now!
Kiss me as if you entered gay
My heart at some noonday,
A bud that dares not disallow
The claim, so all is rendered up,
And passively its shattered cup
Over your head to sleep I bow.

And the sunlight clasps the earth,
    And the moonbeams kiss the sea:
What are all these kissings worth
    If thou kiss not me?

You remind me
define me
incline me.

If you died
I'd.

V

rest

Go to bed late,
Stay very small;
Go to bed early,
Grow very tall.

camomile tea
katherine mansfield

Outside the sky is light with stars;
There's a hollow roaring from the sea.
And, alas! for the little almond flowers,
The wind is shaking the almond tree.

How little I thought, a year ago,
In the horrible cottage upon the Lee
That he and I should be sitting so
And sipping a cup of camomile tea.

Light as feathers the witches fly,
The horn of the moon is plain to see;
By a firefly under a jonquil flower
A goblin toasts a bumble-bee.

We might be fifty, we might be five,
So snug, so compact, so wise are we!
Under the kitchen-table leg
My knee is pressing against his knee.

Our shutters are shut, the fire is low,
The tap is dripping peacefully;
The saucepan shadows on the wall
Are black and round and plain to see.

bed in summer
robert louis stevenson

In winter I get up at night
And dress by yellow candle-light.
In summer, quite the other way,
I have to go to bed by day.

I have to go to bed and see
The birds still hopping on the tree,
Or hear the grown-up people's feet
Still going past me in the street.

And does it not seem hard to you,
When all the sky is clear and blue,
And I should like so much to play,
To have to go to bed by day?

From breakfast on through all the day
At home among my friends I stay,
But every night I go abroad
Afar into the land of Nod.

All by myself I have to go,
With none to tell me what to do –
All alone beside the streams
And up the mountain-sides of dreams.

The strangest things are there for me,
Both things to eat and things to see,
And many frightening sights abroad
Till morning in the land of Nod.

Try as I like to find the way,
I never can get back by day,
Nor can remember plain and clear
The curious music that I hear.

bath
amy lowell

The day is fresh-washed and fair, and there is a smell of tulips and narcissus in the air.

The sunshine pours in at the bath-room window and bores through the water in the bath-tub in lathes and planes of greenish-white. It cleaves the water into flaws like a jewel, and cracks it to bright light.

Little spots of sunshine lie on the surface of the water and dance, dance, and their reflections wobble deliciously over the ceiling; a stir of my finger sets them whirring, reeling. I move a foot and the planes of light in the water jar. I lie back and laugh, and let the green-white water, the sun-flawed beryl water, flow over me. The day is almost too bright to bear, the green water covers me from the too bright day. I will lie here awhile and play with the water and the sun spots. The sky is blue and high. A crow flaps by the window, and there is a whiff of tulips and narcissus in the air.

To fling my arms wide
In some place of the sun,
To whirl and to dance
Till the white day is done.
Then rest at cool evening
Beneath a tall tree
While night comes on gently,
        Dark like me –
That is my dream!

To fling my arms wide
In the face of the sun,
Dance! Whirl! Whirl!
Till the quick day is done.
Rest at pale evening . . .
A tall, slim tree . . .
Night coming tenderly
        Black like me.

A flock of sheep that leisurely pass by,
One after one; the sound of rain, and bees
Murmuring; the fall of rivers, winds and seas,
Smooth fields, white sheets of water, and pure sky;
I have thought of all by turns, and still I lie
Sleepless; and soon the small birds' melodies
Must hear, first uttered from my orchard trees;
And the first cuckoo's melancholy cry.
Even thus last night, and two nights more, I lay,
And could not win thee, Sleep! by any stealth:
So do not let me wear to-night away:
Without Thee what is all the morning's wealth?
Come, blessed barrier between day and day,
Dear mother of fresh thoughts and joyous health!

lights out
edward thomas

I have come to the borders of sleep,
The unfathomable deep
Forest where all must lose
Their way, however straight,
Or winding, soon or late;
They cannot choose.

Many a road and track
That, since the dawn's first crack,
Up to the forest brink,
Deceived the travellers,
Suddenly now blurs,
And in they sink.

Here love ends,
Despair, ambition ends;
All pleasure and all trouble,
Although most sweet or bitter,
Here ends in sleep that is sweeter
Than tasks most noble.

There is not any book
Or face of dearest look
That I would not turn from now
To go into the unknown
I must enter, and leave, alone,
I know not how.

The tall forest towers;
Its cloudy foliage lowers
Ahead, shelf above shelf;
Its silence I hear and obey
That I may lose my way
And myself.

from *macbeth*
william shakespeare

> Innocent sleep:
> Sleep that knits up the ravelled sleeve of care,
> The death of each day's life, sore labour's bath,
> Balm of hurt minds, great nature's second course,
> Chief nourisher in life's feast.

We are such stuff
As dreams are made on, and our little life
Is rounded with a sleep.

Warm summer sun,
    Shine kindly here,
Warm southern wind,
    Blow softly here.
Green sod above,
    Lie light, lie light.
Good night, dear heart,
    Good night, good night.

All you who sleep tonight
Far from the ones you love,
No hand to left or right,
And emptiness above –

Know that you aren't alone.
The whole world shares your tears,
Some for two nights or one,
And some for all their years.

VI

purpose

the balloon of the mind
w. b. yeats

Hands, do what you're bid:
Bring the balloon of the mind
That bellies and drags in the wind
Into its narrow shed.

To rise with gratitude, to find one's
destined sphere, to feel that work
is good, and hold it dear; to take life's
winding road with laughter and with
song, nor grumble at the load, though
way be long . . . To pluck a harmful weed
and plant a blossom there, to see
another's need, his burdens share; to
laugh, and joke a bit, to cherish one true
friend, preserve a gentle wit unto the
end . . . To find in little things one's
greatest happiness, the bird that sweetly
sings, the wind's caress; to reach the
Inn of Rest, and know the day has sped;
to breathe, 'I've done my best' – and
so to bed.

Suppose you're dressed for walking,
  And the rain comes pouring down,
Will it clear off any sooner
  Because you scold and frown?
And wouldn't it be nicer
  For you to smile than pout,
And so make sunshine in the house
  When there is none without?

Oh, humpback of the week,
yardstick of productivity,
all to play for, seesaw pivot
of possibility. Is your gaze
holding mine for fractionally
longer than necessary
a sign of desire or disgust?
Will we even make it
to the weekend together?

Sometimes, Wednesday,
I wonder why I bother.

But then again it's market day
in town, Matt and his fish van
are back – fresh from brain surgery,
his scalp fuzzy with new growth –
and here are plump scallops
glistening on their bed of ice,
and oh Wednesday I think,
come on, let's go for it,
let's be lavish and splash out.

good citizen
a. b.

I vote
I march
I sign
I donate
I post

my protest:

NOT
IN
MY
NAME

i also

sometimes

(mainly when I'm on holiday)

piss in the sea

We, the Fairies, blithe and antic,
Of dimensions not gigantic,
Though the moonshine mostly keep us,
Oft in orchards frisk and peep us.

Stolen sweets are always sweeter,
Stolen kisses much completer,
Stolen looks are nice in chapels,
Stolen, stolen, be your apples.

When to bed the world are bobbing,
Then's the time for orchard-robbing;
Yet the fruit were scarce worth peeling,
Were it not for stealing, stealing.

I celebrate myself, and sing myself,
And what I assume you shall assume,
For every atom belonging to me as good belongs to you.

I loafe and invite my Soul;
I lean and loafe at my ease, observing a spear of
      summer grass . . .

Houses and rooms are full of perfumes – the shelves are
      crowded with perfumes;
I breathe the fragrance myself, and know it and like it;
The distillation would intoxicate me also, but I shall not
      let it.

The atmosphere is not a perfume – it has no taste of the
      distillation – it is odorless;
It is for my mouth forever – I am in love with it;
I will go to the bank by the wood, and become
      undisguised and naked;
I am mad for it to be in contact with me.

Out of the night that covers me,
    Black as the pit from pole to pole,
I thank whatever gods may be
    For my unconquerable soul.

In the fell clutch of circumstance
    I have not winced nor cried aloud.
Under the bludgeonings of chance
    My head is bloody, but unbowed.

Beyond this place of wrath and tears
    Looms but the Horror of the shade,
And yet the menace of the years
    Finds and shall find me unafraid.

It matters not how strait the gate,
    How charged with punishments the scroll,
I am the master of my fate,
    I am the captain of my soul.

I was made erect and lone,
And within me is the bone;
Still my vision will be clear,
Still my life will not be drear,
To the center all is near.
Where I sit there is my throne.
If age choose to sit apart,
If age choose, give me the start,
Take the sap and leave the heart.

from *hamlet*
william shakespeare

This above all: to thine own self be true,
And it must follow, as the night the day,
Thou canst not then be false to any man.

Index of Poems, **Poets** and *First Lines*

Acknowledgements

Maya Angelou, 'Woman Work' from *And Still I Rise* © Maya Angelou 1978. Reprinted by kind permission of Virago, an imprint of Little, Brown Book Group.

Francine Elena, 'On First Sight' © Francine Elena, first published in *The Honest Ulsterman*. Reprinted by kind permission of Francine Elena.

Nikita Gill, 'Forgiveness' from *Wild Embers* © Nikita Gill 2017, published in Great Britain by Trapeze, an imprint of The Orion Publishing Group Ltd.

Nikita Gill, 'Temporary and Permanent' © Nikita Gill. Reprinted by kind permission of The Good Literary Agency.

Adrian Henri, 'Love Is' from the Mersey Sound © Adrian Henri 1967. Reprinted by kind permission of Penguin Books.

Langston Hughes, 'Dream Variations' from *The Collected Poems of Langston Hughes* edited by Arnold Rampersad with David Roessel, Associate Editor. Copyright © 1994 by the Estate of Langston Hughes. Used by permission of Alfred A. Knopf, an imprint of the Knopf Doubleday Publishing Group, a division of Penguin Random House LLC. All rights reserved.

Naomi Jaffa, 'Poem for Wednesday' from *Driver* © Naomi Jaffa (2017, Garlic Press). Reprinted by kind permission of Naomi Jaffa.

Hollie McNish, 'Beautiful' © Hollie McNish. Reprinted by kind permission of Johnson & Alcock.

Vikram Seth Untitled poem from *All You Who Sleep Tonight* © Vikram Seth. Reprinted by kind permission of Vikram Seth.

Lemn Sissay 'Love Poem' from *Rebel Without Applause* (1992, Canongate Ltd). Reprinted by kind permission of Lemn Sissay.

The editor has donated her fee for this volume to the charity Women for Refugee Women: www.refugeewomen.co.uk.

Look at the stars! Look, look up at the skies!
Gerard Manley Hopkins